O[…] of Dunstable

2

Shops & Markets

Fred Moore
Don Kemp

Fred Moore

Don Kemp

Dunstable & District - Local History Society

This series of booklets is being
produced with financial assistance from
Dunstable Town Council, for which the
History Society is grateful.

Published by
Dunstable and District Local History Society

ISBN 0 9529156 1 8

Typeset in *Impression - Style* (Computer Concept Ltd)
Design and layout by Omer Roucoux
and printed by Bartham Press (Watford) Ltd.

CONTENTS

ACKNOWLEDGEMENT

The Society and the authors acknowledge with thanks those people who, in any way, have helped in the production of this book and towards the information it contains. Their assistance and commitment is greatly appreciated.

OUR AUTHORS

Fred Moore was born in Dunstable and has lived in the town virtually all his life. He was educated at Dunstable Grammar School and is a qualified Chartered Accountant. He is the son of the founder, Charles Moore, of Moore's, the department store in the centre of the town. Fred has been highly involved in this shop for well over 50 years and has taken a considerable part in the town's business, service and church life. Fred and his wife, May, have four children (one of whom, Pauline, now runs the shop) and ten grand-children.

Don Kemp was born and bred in Dunstable and has continued to live in the town. He attended the most respected Chiltern Road School, then went to Northfields, where he was one of the very first intake when that school opened in 1936. He joined Charles Arthur Allcorn's business of estate agent, auctioneer and valuer in 1938, returning to the firm after a five year war service in the R.A.F. Later, in the early 1960s, he went into industry and is now retired. Don and his wife, Peggy, have a son and daughter and two grand-children

FOREWORD

This is the second of a series of booklets, published by the Dunstable and District Local History Society, under the title *'Old Trades of Dunstable'* . The first one — *'Dales' Dubbin & Flemons' Herbs'* — was produced in November 1996, and is now out of print. Both books follow presentations made at meetings of the Society, covering former trades and businesses of the town.

As in the first publication, the second book provides fuller and more detailed information than given at the evening presentation, following additional research and further memories of the two authors.

Dunstable for centuries has been a market town, a place of shops and shopkeepers selling a whole variety of goods. It is this aspect that we cover in this particular edition of *'Old Trades of Dunstable'*. We hope that you will enjoy it.

Colin Bourne
Chairman

SHOPS

Fred Moore

Recollections of some of the old shops in Dunstable based on a talk given at a meeting of the Dunstable & District Local History Society on 14th November 1995. The talk took the form of an informal question and answer discussion with the Chairman of the Society and this style is followed here.

Q. Fred, during the period to which you will refer, Dunstable was still very much a country market town, wasn't it?

A. Yes, people came in from the villages – walking, often long distances, cycling, pony and trap, carrier's wagonette. There were no organised, successful buses operated until 1920, and then, I think, only from Luton. These were double deckers with solid tyres and open tops. The conductor had to shout to warn passengers when going under Church Street bridge – "Duck your heads!" I believe there was at least one nasty accident when a passenger did not hear this warning.

There were still farms in the town. Mr. Pratt's was right in the town centre, about where Iceland is now.

An open street market was held on Wednesdays and Saturdays, in High Street North. This extended from outside the 'Nag's Head' on the corner of West Street down to Albion Street. The stalls, stored behind the old Town Hall, of blessed memory, were of solid wood construction with tarpaulin tops and sides and were dismantled for storing. In winter they were lit by naphtha flares.

The Town Council has a notice of 1871 inviting tenders for the construction of six of these stalls. These were doubtless still in use when I was a boy. Whether these stalls were the first of this type to be used or replacements or additions, I do not know. One has quite a good idea of what they looked like from Worthington Smith's well-known sketch of the cross-roads drawn in 1885. We have had this printed on tea towels which have gone all over the world.

The market stalls sold many types of goods – clothing, footwear, china, etc., and were well patronised.

When did Moore's start, and where?

Father came to Dunstable from Bedford at the beginning of 1908, and mother, whom he met at the Bedford shop where they worked, came shortly afterwards when they were married in the March of that year. He took over an existing business in High Street North, next door to Charles Smy, the well known photographer. These were in the row of four shops next to George Street. Mr. Hamilton took over the shop when we moved, then Mr. & Mrs. Wilderspin. It is now occupied by 'Family Affair'. These shops were in quite a good position as George Street led down to the main gate of Waterlow's, which in those days had many hundreds of employees. Mr. Smy must have been one of the very first shops to be lit by electricity for he had his own generator many years before electricity came to the town.

The first Moore's shop in 1916. The four shops, left to right : J.L. Wignell (butcher), which continued to be a butcher's shop for many years ; J.S. Hall (confectionery) ; Moore's, and the photographer, Charles Smy. Two small boys stand on the forecourt — on the left, Fred Moore, on the right, Maurice Smy. The picture is dominated by the magnificent Crossley Motors 20 - 25 h.p. touring car, produced 1914. It was used in the First World War as a staff car, but it also served as a small truck or ambulance. A second car stands behind. *[FTM]*

In January 1917 we moved to High Street South – no. 11 in those days. The houses were numbered consecutively up to the end house on Half Moon Hill and then back to the cross-roads on the other side, so Middle Row shops were from no. 171 by The Square on to 189 by the cross-roads. In 1920 (25th October) shops and houses were all re-numbered – odd numbers our side and evens opposite. We became no. 21.

CHARLES MOORE,

271 High Street N., DUNSTABLE.

GENERAL AND FANCY DRAPERY.

= **Men's and Boys' Clothing.** =

NOTED FOR HARDWEAR HOSIERY.

We make Men's Suits to Measure from 21/- and guarantee to fit you. If you give us a trial you will be assured that we cannot be beaten for Value. Immense Stock of New Seasons Goods now showing.

Advertisement in James Tibbett's Dunstable Almanack & Directory, 1914. [FTM]

Our shop is well over 400 years old and incorporates stones from the Priory after its dissolution under Henry VIII. In a document in 1794 it is described as a cottage in South Street. In a deed of 1804 it was occupied by Richard Underwood, a tailor, who married Ann Darley, sister of John Darley, the founder of Methodism in Dunstable. There were still no numbers, so it was identified as 'formally in the occupation of Edward Shicklethorp, Plumber & Glazier, then James Willoughby and then Francis Saunders'. This would take the occupants well back into the 1700s.

John Darley's son, also a John, inherited the property on the death of his aunt, Ann Underwood and her son, and in 1853 leased it to James Tibbett. Mr. Tibbett had a printing press in one of our cellars and it was here he printed the first Dunstable newspaper, the *Dunstable Chronicle*, the direct ancestor of the *Dunstable Gazette*, which for a great many years was always referred to as the *'Borough Gazette'*. The *Dunstable Chronicle* began as a weekly paper on 5th January 1856.

What type of shop did you have then?

The style of fittings and stock was very different in those days. I believe, very early on, in common with other shops, there was no covering on the floor boards.

Then came lino, saving the problem of dust. Lighting was by gas, hissing away when it was dark, as electricity did not come to Dunstable until 1925. I don't think the gas lights were lit until dusk, so the shops could get pretty gloomy, particularly if it was a dull day. All possible stock was kept in drawers – first, solid wood ; later, glass fronted and light oak. The counters were long, painted wood base and mahogany tops. Later came glass counters. There were high bentwood chairs for the customers' comfort while the assistants brought a selection of the articles requested for a choice to be made. There was no self-service and no items were pre-packed. All the drapers kept large stocks of piece goods – coating, dress materials, sheeting – bleached, unbleached or flannelette, none in colours or patterns. Winceyette for nightwear and petticoats, towelling curtain material and curtain nets - long and short. Mantelpiece borders, table cloths – chenille, velveteen, etc. Door curtains to keep out the draughts, chenille or plushette. A lot of thick clothing – wool, wool plated, fleecy lined vests and pants, lined shirts, Derby tweed suits, Moleskin and Melton trousers for the men, fleecy lined underwear for the ladies, and combinations for men, women and children. All types of warm stockings were sold that are not seen nowadays – wool, silk and wool, and thick lisle (mercerised cotton) both fully fashioned and seamless; no nylons appeared until after the last war. And people all wore gloves in those days. Kid (leather) - fur backed and all lined – fur, wool, fleece or silk and astrakhan and wool gloves worn for the winter, and for the summer, unlined kid or fabric.

During the last war when normal stocks were very difficult to get and clothing coupons did not go very far, we sold thousands of linen flour bags which people put to all manner of uses – tea towels, tablecloths, and even sheets. Also several hundredweights of cotton dish cloth yarn for many kinds of knitted goods, both these items being coupon free. A very large quantity of frilling in various colours was also sold for collars and cuffs of ladies dresses to rejuvenate them – quite a morale booster when coupons had run out.

The hours were long :

Monday to Wednesday....	9am to 7pm
Thursday, early closing	9am to 1pm

(This was enforced by law – one shop was fined for dressing its window in the afternoon)

Fridays....	9am to 8pm, ½hr. for tea
Saturdays	9am to 9pm, ½hr. for tea

Shops closed from 1 o'clock to 2 o'clock for lunch. All the assistants worked these hours, there were no shifts or part-timers. No shops opened on Sundays and blinds or shutters were pulled down.

There were no perpetual sales, the winter sale was in January and the summer sale in August. There was healthy but not cut throat competition. This ensured that the prices were reasonable and really the businesses relied on giving good service, with courtesy, and their reputation for fair dealing to attract customers. As far as I know they all made a living. Prices are difficult to visualise now. In 1914 father advertised tailor made suits, 'guaranteed to fit' for 21/- (£1.05) and shirts for 3/6d (17½ p). In the 1920s he advertised dresses 2/11d (15p) to 18/11d (95p). In the 1930s corsets 3/11½d (20p) and artificial silk stockings 1/11¾d (10p). These prices and the prices quoted later seem to us incredibly cheap, but all the shopkeepers were of good repute and the goods were all of reliable quality.

The shop at no. 21 High Street South, before alteration and expansion. As far as is known Moore's is the oldest retail shop in Dunstable still in the same family and also the last family shop started before the First World War still in existence. [FTM]

Who were your neighbours in those days?

In common with the great majority of shopkeepers we lived on the premises. Our living quarters were quite commodious, eight rooms plus the usual offices and a long walled garden. On one side we had the Tibbetts, whose business was founded in 1840. They sold gifts, stationery and books, china, glass and earthenware; a very interesting old shop and house, with a large garden. They had the Index Printing Works behind the shop and later, under Cyril Tibbett, this became a very large concern extending over all their garden, the bottom part of ours and the International Stores paddock. Index specialised in time-tables, including the famous A.B.C. Rail Guide. After the last war Cyril started the ABC World Airways Guide, which became of international repute, Shipping, Coach and other travel-related Guides. In 1923 they sold the shop to Boots the Chemists and when Boots moved to The Quadrant we bought the premises for our fashion and childrens wear departments.

Tibbett's shop in the early 1920s [JT]

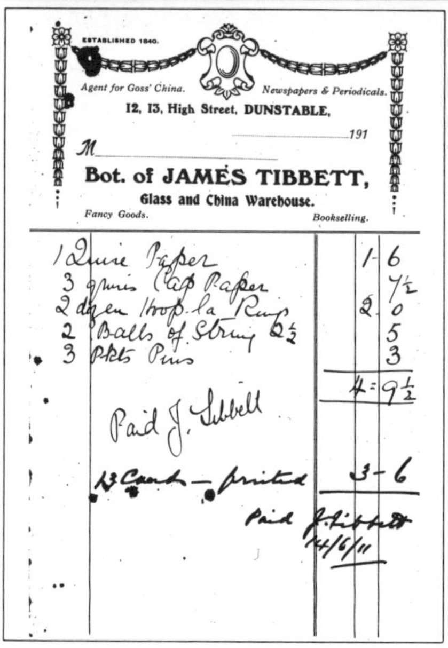
ESTABLISHED 1840.

Agent for Goss' China. Newspapers & Periodicals.

12, 13, High Street, DUNSTABLE, 191

M

Bot. of JAMES TIBBETT,

Glass and China Warehouse.

Fancy Goods. Bookselling.

1 Quire Paper	1	6
3 Quires Cap Paper		7½
2 dozen Hoop la Rings	2	0
2 Balls of String 2½		5
3 Pkts Pins		3
	4	9½
Paid J. Tibbett		
13 Cards – printed	3	6
Paid J. Tibbett 14/6/11		

On the other side was Joseph Andrews – 'The Victoria Bun House' – a high class baker and pastrycook. His madeira cake with a slice of peel on top was unequalled. The bakehouse in those days was under the shop and the most appetising smells used to waft up on to the pavement and into our shop. One of Mr. Andrew's advertisements stated 'Wedding cakes a speciality – exquisitely decorated from 1/6d [7½p] a pound'. Joseph Andrews was Mayor of Dunstable 1922 - 23.

A Tibbett invoice dated 14th June, 1911. Note that the third item, costing 2s 0d, is for 2 doz. Hoop la Rings.

Fred, I believe there was an occasion, wasn't there, when Mr. & Mrs. Andrews carried a very large tiered anniversary cake across the High Street to the Methodist church across the way ?

Yes, the traffic was stopped!

Next door to the Victoria Bun House was the International Stores. Mr. Ludlow was the Manager and our families were great friends. The Stores had a large garden with a beautiful copper beech tree, and a paddock which went behind the gardens of Mr. Andrews and ours and overlooked the garden of Mr. Munt, who lived at the Priory House and who seemed to be a very stern looking man. The Ludlows had a mulberry tree in the paddock which was reputed to go back to the days of the Priory before its dissolution. A pre-1914 advertisement of the Stores shows Ceylindo tea at 1/6d (7½p) a lb. The International made deliveries in the town and the villages by horse and covered van. There was no self-service in the shop and there were different counters for different types of goods and a lot of work for the staff. Sugar came in bulk and was bagged up in blue bags. Bacon

c.1920. The staff of the International Stores line up outside, together with the shop's horse and delivery van. An elderly lady stands at the entrance to Church Walk below an advertisement for Wills' Golden Virginia & Honey Cut tobacco. Mr. Boskett's shop (described in the text later, along with the adjacent two shops) can just be seen, far left. Woolworth's now occupy the site of the shops immediately left of the alley and the International is now a betting shop. [DG] came in sides, and was cut and sliced to the thickness the customer required. Whole cheeses were on the counter and cut with the wire cheese cutter. Lard was cut, weighed and wrapped in greaseproof paper. Butter was knocked up with butterpats into artistic patterns. Biscuits were sold loose from large square tins and the broken biscuits sold off cheaply. These three shops were our immediate neighbours and we were all very good friends.

What about the other shops nearby?

Apart from the International Stores there were very few multiples in the town and except for World Stores, which had a nameplate with gold lettering on a blue glass background, and the British and Argentine Meat Co. in High Street North, they were all on our side of the cross-roads. There was no Co-op in the town when I was a boy.

As Joan Curran mentioned in her most interesting article in our History Society's Newsletter no. 4 *'Looking back to 1914'*, there was an extraordinary variety and number of shops for such a small town.

On our side of High Street South, beginning at the cross-roads, there was the Home & Colonial Tea Stores (but which sold much more than tea) with the highly polished brass nameplate on the front and sawdust on the floor. Indeed, all shops were well maintained – brass and copper shone, windows sparkled, the pavement swept daily and washed down regularly. Snow was cleared, which we dare not do now, for if a little piece of ice is left and a pedestrian slips on it we can be sued for damages. Next door to the Home & Colonial was Freeman, Hardy & Willis, for boots and shoes. Both these shops were demolished when Church Street was widened, together with 'The Red Lion' on the other side of Church Street. Then came Foster Bros. – men's and boys' clothing, now Pet's World.

Percy Ashwell was next at no. 7 for ladies wear. His shop was always painted white, which stood out because nearly all shops were of a dark colour. Before coming to Dunstable Mr. Ashwell was with Hitchcock Williams & Co., a very large, old established wholesale warehouse of high repute in St. Paul's Churchyard. The interest to me is that the Mr. Williams was the founder of the YMCA, which has done so much over the years for many thousands of young men. To start off with at Dunstable Mr. Ashwell was at no. 1, before selling it to the Home & Colonial, but by 1917 he had moved to no. 7, which had been Lockhart's.

As Lockhart & Son this shop had a very long history, being founded in 1840. This must have been the largest shop in the town up to the early 1900s. It went through to Church Street, where Gibbs & Dandy were later, and had a 'live-in' staff. They were high-class 'Drapers and Silk Mercers' and had a very large

Where to Shop at Dunstable.

A Corner of The New Furniture Gallery.

CHARLES LOCKHART & SON,

Silk Mercers, Tailors, House Furnishers.

General Drapers, Outfitters, Carpet Factors.

AND FUNERAL CARRIAGE PROPRIETORS.

ESTABLISHED 1840.

3 & 4, High St., 2, 3 & 4, Church St., DUNSTABLE.

CHARLES LOCKHART & SON'S DRESSMAKING AND COSTUME DEPARTMENT is under the management of a Fitter who has had West End Experience, and is able to carry out ANY orders entrusted to her.

C. L. & SON also execute all classes of UPHOLSTERING, FITTING BLINDS, PLANNING CARPETS AND LINOLEUM, REMOVING OR WAREHOUSING FURNITURE; and submit Estimates for all Requirements.

A New Feature is the **SERIES OF FURNISHED ROOMS**, which are arranged for the Assistance of Purchasers.

ALL GOODS DELIVERED FREE.

[WGS]

furniture department. They had a large trade in mourning wear, for everyone in the family wore black when there was a bereavement. Also they were Funeral Directors. Mr. Melville Lockhart, the last of that branch of the Lockhart family, was with Mr. Ashwell for many years. He was one of the old school, always formally dressed in black coat, grey waistcoat, striped trousers, and of great integrity. He served at the front in the Great War as a non-combatant on medical field work, and won several decorations for gallantry. He exercised great influence at the Methodist Church, particularly among the young men.

'Uncle' Melville, as he was known, disliked being involved in the funeral procession, but I believe Percy Ashwell was in his element leading the cortege. On these occasions Percy was naturally serious, but normally he was a cheerful, extrovert personality. As with very many shopkeepers with their wives, he was ably assisted in the business by Mrs. Ashwell, who was the sister of Frank Herington, the pharmacist. It therefore seems appropriate that Herington's later moved into these premises when Gibbs & Dandy, who took them over from Mr. Ashwell, left the town.

Like most of us drapers, Lockhart's had a lot of customers in the villages. They ran a big 'club' and in the autumn they would bring the villagers in from all around by wagonette to spend their club money. If the money was paid in for the whole year it earned a bonus of 3/- in the £, quite a consideration.

Next was Mr. Tompkins, a boot and shoe maker, established before 1890. No wonder a lot of these shopkeepers looked old men to me as a young boy! Mr. Tomkins always hung a lot of footwear outside the shop, reaching from the top of the window to the pavement. This is now the Electric Shop.

Next door was Mr. F.W. Boskett, father of Leslie Boskett, who was a master at the Grammar School and a gifted musician and Organist and Choirmaster at the Methodist Church, The Square. Mr. Boskett had a double fronted shop selling pianos and music. Up a step towards the back of the shop was the Middle Row sub-Post Office. A curious combination!

No. 13 (new numbering) was Mr. J.S. Bowles. This looked a very old shop front painted black with fairly small windows, selling clocks, watches and jewellery. Then Mr. P.J. Green, established 1887, a tobacconist. This had a lovely smell of tobacco and cigars which made it an irresistible temptation to take up smoking. He also had a good stock of Goss china bearing the Dunstable Coat of Arms. He sold the business later to Bales and it was run by Jack Rice, who became very well-known in the town. I don't know what they did behind but, generally speaking, if you went in, they came from the back to serve you. Some owners didn't seem to wait in the shop a lot in those days if trade was quiet, unless of course they had an assistant who would be there all the time.

P.J. Green, 'Stationer and Fancy Repository', 'Wholesale and Retail Tobacconist' *[JT]*

So you walked into the shop and there was nobody there? The proprietor, or the shopkeeper, suddenly appeared from the back and served you?

That's right. A bell over the door gave warning of your approach. That even applied to Percy Lester opposite, who was a jeweller. He used to walk in the shop after the bell had gone. It was all very trusting.

The next four businesses I have already mentioned as our neighbours and ourselves. Then came Mr. F.P. Walker, later Ropers, another boot and shoe shop, Harry Pratt's antiques shop, and Mr. Frank Herington, the chemist, the business being founded by his father in 1887. Frank told me that when living at the shop as a boy, playing with his hoop, a sight never seen nowadays, the policeman told him to play in the road, saying - "It isn't safe for pedestrians on the pavements!" In those days grass grew on the High Street. As mentioned earlier the business has now moved nearer to the cross-roads and is owned by Mr. Gerald Fox.

Next door, at no. 33, in my boyhood, was a nice old red-brick house occupied by Mr. A.N. Gutteridge. This was later partly converted into a ladies fashion area, with the addition of a tasteful shop front, where Mrs. Room, who lived in the house with her family, carried out some excellent dressmaking work to a wide clientele. After Mrs. Room retired, Mr. & Mrs. Mead ran it for many years as the very popular Priory Café. It is now an Indian restaurant.

On the other side of Priory House was Mr. Fowler's grocer's shop. His sons founded the well-known firm of Fowler's Jams at Watford. This was another old shop, which one stepped down into from the road and was greeted by an appetising aroma of coffee stored on shelves in large black and gold tins. When I remember it, the shop was run by Mr. George King, who had married Mr. Fowler Snr's daughter.

Then Scott's Garage, founded in 1882 by Mr. W. Scott, in those days selling bicycles, before cars were introduced. This became the largest garage in Dunstable, also with showrooms. Mr. Ben Scott sold the writer his first motor car, belonging to Dr. Binns – a Morris – for £35! Mr. Scott was Mayor of Dunstable from 1952 - 54. During the last war he was responsible for dealing with the petrol rationing coupons for commercial and farm vehicles for the district – time consuming, but unpaid. After Scott's came Harry Rixson's, a lovely old shop and house, full of fine antiques. These shops are now demolished and replaced by post-war style shops.

The other side of 'The Saracens Head', in a small row of shops that still exist in some form and which included Mr. Boxford, baker and pastrycook, was that of Mr. Watts – newsagent, barber and hairdresser. Mr. Watts, who was fully occupied in the saloon behind the shop, was known as the 'Demon Barber' for his lively action when cutting hair or shaving. All shaving was done with a cut-throat razor.

Further up High Street South, at the corner of Britain Street, was Mr. England's bakery. Both Mr. England's sons, Fred and Bert, and all his daughters were well-known in the town. Mr. Frank Kenworthy, who came to Dunstable as a soldier in the Great War, married Mr. England's daughter, Gertrude, and worked in the business for some time. He later moved to West Street, building a furniture store on the site of some old property. He took an active part in Civic life, serving as Mayor 1936 - 37. On the opposite corner was Mr. Alfred Cook. He took over his sister's grocery and greengrocery shop, ably assisted by Mrs. Cook. After a while he used premises at the back for selling second-hand furniture. Later he gave up the food side, putting in a new front shop and selling new furniture in the front, the second-hand department still being at the rear. He was also involved in the Civic life of Dunstable and was Mayor for four successive years 1932 - 36. Alfred Cook was one of the personalities of Dunstable. His son, Harold, joined him in the business before the last war and rejoined after being invalided out of the Armed Forces until ill health caused him to retire in 1956.

Middle Row, opposite you, Fred – can we know about that?

This is a very interesting row with some of the buildings, according to the W.E.A. Chronicle of 1986, reputed to go back to the first half of the 14th century.

These make up the original medieval Market Hall. The corner building, next to The Square, now the Imperial Cancer Research Charity Shop, I remember as the London Central Meat Co., later Baxter's. This is not very interesting architecturally, but has deeds going back to the time of Charles II. Next, no. 36, was Mr. Harry Menear's Dining Rooms, now G.B. News. No. 34, Donald McLeod Gibbs, tailor, then for many years occupied by Stoten's the hairdresser after they had moved from no. 32. Mr. Henry Stoten had two sons – Bill, who ran the men's saloon in the front and Albert, the ladies in the room behind. No. 32, Chas. Boskett, hairdresser and perfumer and repairer of umbrellas, later Mr. Stotens before he moved next door to no. 34 and the premises were acquired, in 1934, by A.E. Fisher, the butcher, for one of his shops. He carried on the business there for many years. Now it is 'Going Places'. No. 30 was the home of the Singer Sewing Machine Co., from the early years of the century until the 1940s. Outside this shop hung the Singer sign with the famous big 'S' on it.

No. 28, Ann Young's, was a very old shop front with small panes of glass and entered by two or three outside steps up from the pavement. The family were here before 1840 and were grocers. Ann was reputed to be a good friend to the families in the cottages in the area behind – Ashton Street, Prosperous Row and Chapel Walk. She acted as unofficial nurse and dispensed her home-made remedies. She is also remembered as a dressmaker. I think by the time I was around she had given up the groceries. Ann died in 1921, when the shop was modernised and became Hooton's Penny Bazaar. They closed in the mid-thirties, and later David Sewell opened his fish shop here. He also had a fried fish and chip shop behind in Back (Ashton) Street. I remember seeing large blocks of ice being delivered to keep the fish fresh – no cold storage in those days.

He sold a great variety of fish, didn't he?

He did; he is reputed to have sold 30 commercial varieties of fish, but his favourite was still cod.

No. 26 was Eastman's, the butchers, now 'Cooks Collection'. No. 24 was the Misses Gaisford, ladies and childrens wear. They moved to West Street in 1923 and Mr. John Buckle opened his menswear shop. Suits were made to measure on the premises. John always sold good quality clothes and was very popular. Overcoats were advertised 45/- to 105/-, suits £4/10/-. On John's retirement his son, Philip, carried on for some time and it is still a good quality menswear shop, now run by John Butterton.

No. 22 was Mr. Cornelius Vater's furniture shop, rebuilt after he suffered a disastrous fire on Boxing Day 1893. On his retirement Mr. Bert Stott bought the business and continued it as a furniture shop, moving from the shop across the

In October 1927 the town held a very successful shopping festival, well supported by the tradespeople and the town folk and with competitions and events. A sign for this can be seen over Mr. Buckle's gentleman's outfitter's shop in Middle Row. *[PJB]*

road which his father had taken over from Mr. Boskett in 1927. This shop was bought by Woolworth's, who also bought Mr. Bowles' shop and replaced them with a new building. Later still they acquired Bales, the tobacconist and again rebuilt. Thus we lost another very old building. Many will remember the half-timbered first floor jutting over Church Walk. Mr. Stott's is now F.L. Moore's, no relation to us, and Mr. Beverley Stott, the grandson of the founder, runs the furniture business from Bull Pond Lane.

No. 20 - Lunaria - was Mr. Brownlow's, who was a grocer and had an off-licence. He advertised whiskies from 3/6d to 4/6d (17p to 22p) and Cockburns Port 3/- (15p). The Misses Emma and Clara Janes ran no. 18 when I was a boy, selling greengrocery and home made jams, marmalade and pickles. The family established this business in 1862. On their retirement Mr. George Gadd, the greengrocer, bought the business and I remember him bringing up stock from the cellar – an excellent cold store.

There was a series of cellars, dark places, which I knew because I was very friendly as a boy with John Gadd, the second son. Did all the shops thereabouts have cellars?

Yes, I believe they did. In our case we had two under no. 21 and one going the full length of no. 23.

To continue, many will remember the long queues George Gadd had outside his shop when bananas returned after the last war. No. 16 was another grocer's shop run by Mr. Frank Sanders and later Mr. Smith, recently 'Jacky's Pantry', then 'The Phone Box'. Many will remember Mr. Percy Lester, the jeweller and silversmith, at no. 14. His father, Walter, started the business in or before 1876, when it was at the corner of West Street and before the premises were knocked down to widen the road. Percy sold the business to Walker's, who moved down to the Quadrant when it was opened and the original shop is now 'The Dogs Bowl'.

No. 12, Mr. J. Howard, another fishmonger, is now knocked down on the ground floor and makes a wide passageway through to Ashton Square. No. 8, originally 'The Swan with Two Necks', was Reynold Cook's haircutting and shaving saloon. He also repaired umbrellas. A German helmet, presumably acquired in the Great War, was on display on the window ledge. This later became Redrup and Starkings, the Luton pastrycooks, and is now Ladbrokes. No. 6 was Ann Wildman's – another greengrocer. Some will remember the dried brown locust beans which children bought to eat on the way to school. This was acquired by Mr. R.J. Blindell, shoe retailer, when it was found the building was unsafe and had to be rebuilt. It is now owned by T & P Stationers who took over from Mr. & Mrs. Burgess.

No. 4 was George Costin's. He was there before 1890, in business as a butcher; in fact this had been a butchers shop since 1840. The slaughter house was behind in Hampton Court, a very impressive name. He also owned horse drawn vehicles – wagonettes, etc. They took the Sunday School children to Ashridge for their annual outings and horse-drawn traps took the Methodist Local Preachers to their Sunday appointments in the surrounding villages. I well remember going in these with my father. He also in due course ran coaches — Costin's Coaches were very well-known. His son Arthur took over this side of the business and Arthur's son, Keith, still has a coach business. The butcher's shop was later run by Tilley's – father, son Vic, and grandson Michael, Town Mayor 1990 - 91 and is now 'Use Your Loaf' – bakers and pastrycooks. In Mr. Tilley Snr's time a good weekly order came to 10/- (50p). At the corner of Middle Row and West Street, no. 2, was Mr. Edwards,

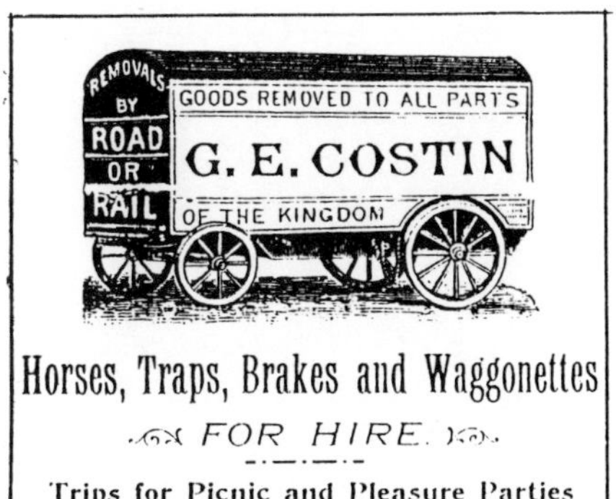

[K]

another draper. He was succeeded by Mr. Keep, who ran the shop as a newsagent and tobacconist. It is now occupied by Taylor's Estate Agents, but still often called 'Keep's Corner'.

What about the other shops in the town centre?

There were so many other interesting shops in the town deserving mention that it is difficult to cover them all other than those which impressed me. In West Street there was Gus Ellis, hairdresser and barber, with his son, Bert. This was a very old building, reputed to be 15th century, next to the Ashton almshouses. It was built before the days of chimneys and had a hole in the roof to allow the smoke from the fire to escape. The fireplace was built later on a foundation of stones from either the Priory or the Friary. This building is now in the Chiltern Open Air Museum awaiting re-erection.

In 1928 Arthur Ward and Archie Hubbard came to no. 13A – a newly built, double fronted shop, with offices above, and opened their electrical business to meet the growing demand for electrical installations in the private homes, shops and offices previously lit by gaslight or oil lamps. Mr. Hubbard was engaged on the outside work and Mr. Ward was in the shop selling kettles, irons, lighting fitments, cookers and fires. In between serving customers he worked in his little office.keeping the books and running the business.

A little farther up, at no. 21, was Braznell's, the fruiterers and greengrocers, and also fresh fish merchants. They always had a big display on the forecourt in front of the shop. Nearby Mr. Frank Kenworthy, mentioned earlier, set up his new shop. On his sudden, untimely death his son, Harold, ran the furniture side and his eldest daughter, Joyce, the china department. At the corner of Cross Street West, a small street which joined St. Mary's Street and West Street, was Mr. Edwin Ayres, who made the real and incomparable Dunstable doughnut – small and crisp. On the opposite side at the corner of Matthew Street was Mr. E.F. Sayer, the butcher. Hanging outside at Christmas time were rows of rabbits, hares, game and several sides of beef. The meat was killed in the slaughterhouse behind the shop. When he retired, Mr. F.B. Longley bought the business. One of his specialities was pork sausages selling at 11½p (5p) a lb.

Next to Mr. V.P. Billett's shoe repairing shop was Miss Capell's confectionery shop, a very popular port of call on Saturday evenings. Miss Capell always seemed to be dressed in old style black silk dresses, but was a delightful and very pleasant lady. At no. 8 was S. Farmer & Co's music shop, selling pianos and

Ward and Hubbard's electrical business lit up for the coronation of King George VI and Queen Elizabeth, 12th May 1937. [YW]

Mr. Sayer, butcher, with a full complement of staff and, seemingly, a full complement of produce . . . *[JT]*

organs, run by Mr. & Mrs. L.E. Wilkes. Mr. Wilkes was a familiar figure cycling round to many homes to tune their pianos. Many folk will remember Farmer's in Church Street and on their move to there the Co-op had their first shop in Farmer's old premises.

In High Street North, just round the corner at no. 7, Mr. Arthur White had his butcher's business in an old style shop entered by two or three steps next to the former 'Crown' public house. This was actually started by his wife who at the same time brought up a family of thirteen children while Arthur farmed at Sewell. His son, Ernest, then carried on the business, being known as 'The Sausage King of Dunstable'! At twenty stone he was a good advertisement for the quality of his meat. Lower down, beyond the old Town Hall, was Mr. F.T. Garrett, 'Watch & Clockmaker and Manufacturing Electrician', who was already in business in 1876. A lot of the stock was fascinating and looked as if it had been there for years. Mr. Garrett was Mayor of Dunstable over three periods, 1897 - 98, 1905 and 1913 - 15, giving many years of service to the town. To a boy, Mr. Garrett was a very dignified, elderly gentleman, with a distinguished looking, pointed, waxed moustache.

Next to Mr. Garrett was Mr. G.A. Waller, the pork butcher, well-known for his delicious pork pies. At no. 33 was Mr. F. Monk and his son Freddie, the drapers widely known for their large stocks of piece goods piled up to the very high ceiling. One of their advertisements quoted coat serges from 1/0¾d (5p) to 6/11d

(35p) a yard. Jackets and mantles were 4/11d (25p) - 29/6d (147½p) and moreen and felt skirts 1/11½p (10p) - 8/11d (45p). Close by, near Albion Street, was Mr. Robinson, the 'Hardware Man'. Mr. W.H. Robinson was another Mayor of Dunstable, 1954 - 56.

On the opposite corner of Albion Street and the High Street at no. 39 were the premises of Mr Miles Taylor. In the shop at the front he sold stationery and had a circulating library. Outside by the door was a very large white enamel thermometer advertising Stephens Ink, identical to the one which had been outside Mr. Tibbett's shop at no. 23 High Street South until the shop was altered. The thermometer at no. 39 had been a well known landmark, often referred to, particularly in hot or cold weather, for very many years until it was vandalised in the 1960s.

Mr. Taylor came to the town to take over the *Dunstable Borough Gazette* after the former proprietor, Mr. Henry Ballans, died in 1895, and he very soon made a great impact on the life of Dunstable. The *Gazette* was produced in the premises behind the shop and the living accommodation was on the third floor. Increasing blindness forced Mr. Taylor to retire in 1928, and after a short ownership by Mr. C.W. Clarke, the *Gazette* and the premises were acquired by Messrs. Gibbs Bamforth & Co., now trading as Home Counties Newspapers, the proprietors of the *Luton News*, etc. The shop was still run as a stationers until the 1960s and the premises used by the Gazette's editorial and advertisement staff until the 1980s.

Further along, just before the old Post Office, was a row of shops at the Manor House. Mr. Josiah Westnutt opened one of these as an electrical shop when electricity came to the town in 1925. His daughter, Mrs. Olive Leach, ran the shop and Mr. Westnutt and his son had the workroom behind and did all the outside electrical work.

Horace Small had his furniture shop in this block and Mr. W.G. Creamer, baker and pastrycook, also had a branch here, the bakery being in Edward Street after moving from Waterlow Road. Mr. Creamer was noted for his excellent bread which won many national and international awards. When Mr. Creamer retired, the business was run equally successfully by Harold West, who had been with him for many years, and his wife, Gladys. The business is now carried on by Mr. Bechert at the premises in Edward Street and still trading as 'W.G. Creamer'. The new Post Office, a very unattractive post-war building and now closed, was later built on the site of these shops.

I think these shops would be the limit of the town centre, but there were several interesting establishments beyond this point. Freddie Brookes had his thriving butcher's shop opposite the Grammar School. He was always bright and jolly and enjoyed a friendly chat with all his customers. One did not have to be in a hurry when buying the weekly joint etc.! At no. 103 Mr. E.J. Potton owned his

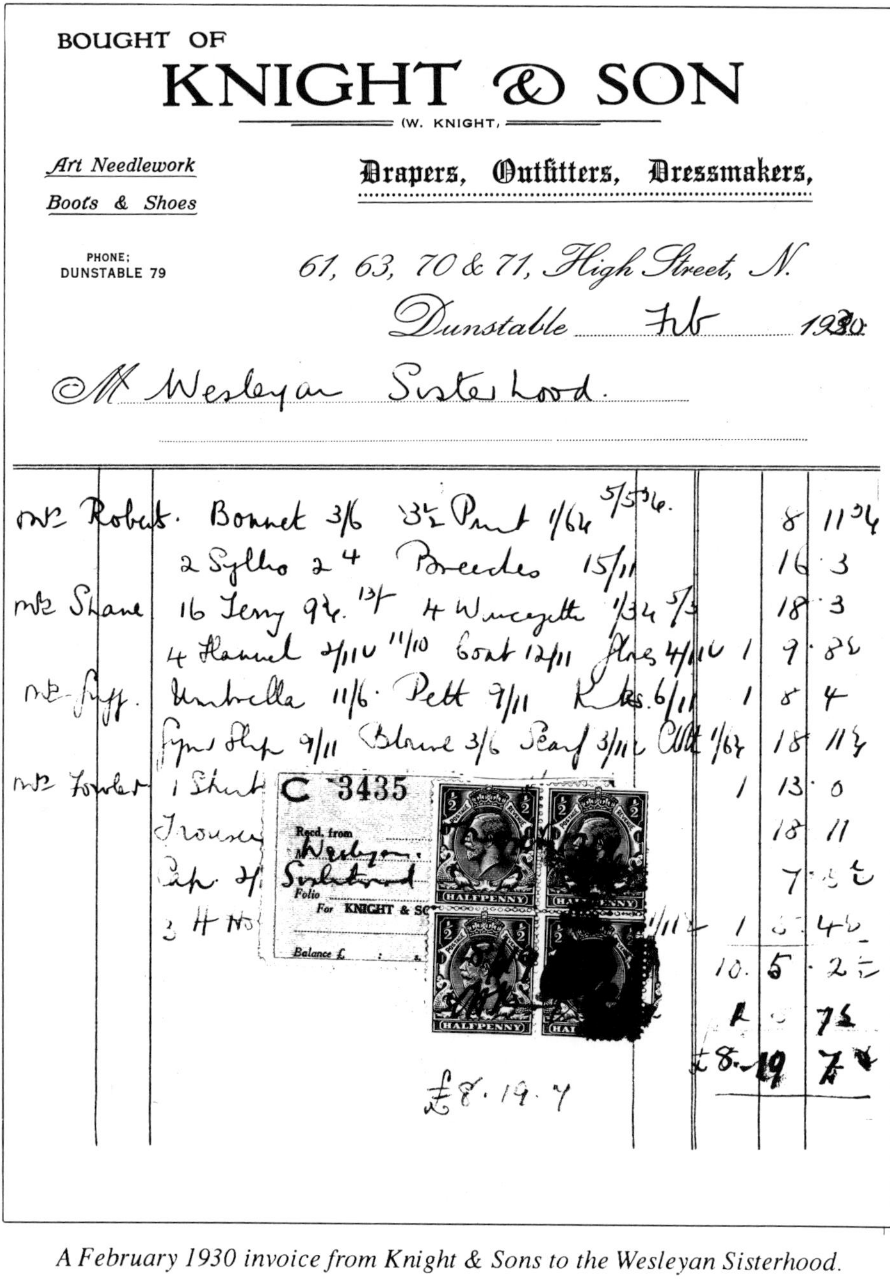

BOUGHT OF

KNIGHT & SON

(W. KNIGHT)

Art Needlework

Boots & Shoes

Drapers, Outfitters, Dressmakers,

PHONE;
DUNSTABLE 79

61, 63, 70 & 71, High Street, N.

Dunstable Feb 1930

M Wesleyan Sisterhood.

C 3435

Recd. from Wesleyan Sisterhood

Folio

For KNIGHT & SON

Balance £ : :

HALFPENNY

£8.19.7

A February 1930 invoice from Knight & Sons to the Wesleyan Sisterhood.

saddlery and harness shop. When he retired J. Wild & Sons of Luton took the shop and, moving with changing conditions, ran it as a very popular sport and leather goods shop, managed by Mr. Sammy Taylor.

Then, of course, Colin, there was your own father's grocery shop at no. 131, which is so vividly described in your own book, *'Bourne & Bred'*, along with others in this part of the town. This shop was owned by Mr. Ernest Mowse before Mr. E.C. Bourne, who, like many others, was a man of absolute integrity, bought it. Next door Mr. John Abell opened his wireless business. For many years before the villages and even many in the town had electricity, he could be seen going round in his motor cycle and side-car, collecting accumulators to be re-charged and returned for a very small cost. The shop, which later sold television sets, still trades under the same name.

Opposite, at the corner of Ashton Road, was Flinte House, a clothing and outfitting business trading as Campbell, Graves & Cox. Mrs. Cox was a well-known personality in the town. Just a little further on there were a few shops fronted by a big forecourt. These included Mr. J.H. Proverbs, stationer and printer, later run by his son-in-law, George Parsons, another well-known personality, a keen singer and long-time member of the Luton Choral Society. The printing works behind the shop was in great demand for printing programmes and posters for the large number of events always being held in the town by the churches and the many organisations.

Next to the Grammar School were two very old shops entered by steps down from the pavement. One was known as the school tuck shop, run by Mr. Foster and later Mr. Barnes, and the other a chemist's owned by Mr. Charles Hinton, who also practised as a dentist, having his surgery next to Chas. Smy's shop. Mr. Hinton was a well-known figure about the town, tall and lean, always wearing a Homburg hat and a prominent member of the pre-war Operatic Society and the Three Arts Club. As mentioned recently in the *Gazette*, he had been born in Kimberley, was a god-son of Cecil Rhodes and had an adventurous career, including serving in the Royal Medical Corps at Gallipoli in the First World War.

On the other side of the High Street, next to Dr. Binns' lovely home, 'The Lawns', in a group of flint faced shops, was the barber, 'Tammy' Barber, looking very spruce and professional with his waxed moustache. In one advertisement in an early Dunstable Year Book, Mr. Barber advertises 'scissors ... ground on the premises ... razor edges guaranteed – price 1d per pair upwards – Straw workers please note'. The general price for a haircut was 6d (2½p) for men and 4d for boys. When electric cutters came in the charge was 8d. Shaving, which many men had done was 3d (1¼p). Mr. Frank Anderson had the high class tailor's shop, established in 1859, where the Grammar School boys purchased the school uniform.

Mr. Walter Knight had a large draper's shop, fascinating for children because of the overhead cash railway from the counters to the cash desk. Next to Walter Knight was Mr. William Durrant's large furniture store. Mr. Durrant's two sons, William and Cyril, and William's daughter, Alston (Holloway) were all in the business. Durrant's served the town for nearly 100 years. The advertisement in Worthington Smith's *History of Dunstable*, published in 1904, features 'Linoleum and floorcloths, China, Earthenware, Lamps, Hardware, Mangles and Machines' and all the lamps featured in the photograph are oil lamps.

'Stop Here for Value' states William Durrant, the 'Complete House Furnisher'. This picture is of Mr. Durrant's old shop, on the west side of the High Street, before he moved across the road to be next to Knight's. *[WGS]*

Further along, past 'The Sugar Loaf' hotel and tap and the other side of the archway where Oxfam now resides, was the Misses Eleanor and Lizzie Wilson's hat shop. Close to the Central Café, they moved to this shop from higher up after the ground floor of the Woolley Sanders hat factory had been converted into shops. Mr. Reg Geary's father started the Central Café in 1927 and was responsible for influencing the well-known Standerwick coaches and other long distance coaches to make it their official stop for refreshments on their journeys to and from London. This brought a great deal of trade to the Central Café and also to the

Whipsiderry in the same block. Many photographs exist showing long lines of coaches parked in that part of the High Street.

Further towards the cross-roads and next to the 'White Hart' was Mr. Joseph Flemons' Pharmacy*, established in 1881. It had an interesting old shop front and the shop was entered by going down one or two steps from the pavement. This, with so many other interesting old shops and buildings, has been demolished to make way for the new shopping development.

Charlie Cole, the well-known racing cyclist, and still racing well into his eighties, moved into his shop, formerly the Misses Wilsons' hat shop before they moved lower down and now the Nationwide premises, from his former shop in West Street. The 'Penny Farthing' over the doorway was a well-known landmark. Next door at no. 18, just before Barclays Bank, was the Confectionery Bazaar, a very popular high class shop run by Miss Rose Harlow and Miss Annie Omer, who had started it sometime before 1904. Their 'real old Edinburgh rock' was a great favourite and their Kunzle and Fullers cakes a real treat. On their retirement Miss Joan MacKenzie ran it for some years until her retirement.

Where Lloyds Bank now is was a large double fronted ironmonger's shop approached by some steps up from the pavement, protected by a handrail. This was run by Mr. Woods, but had belonged to the Chambers family, the two Miss Chambers of whom ran Aberfeldy School, in one of the large houses that used to stand between the old Post Office and Regent Street. Aberfeldy School was next to the former Gas showrooms and offices, built about 1937 on the site of an old Georgian house which the Gas Company had previously used. The ironmonger's shop must have been one of the oldest businesses in Dunstable, being established in 1763.

Then there were two interesting old shops – Mrs. Rose Vickery, who must have been a real chain smoker, selling china, glass and earthenware (earthenware seems to have been a feature with all the china shops) and Mr. Wm. R. Gibbard, the corn merchant. Both these shops were established in 1885. It was from a window above one of these shops that Worthingon Smith made his drawing of the cross roads that I referred to earlier.

In Church Street, on the northern side, was Sam Priest's cycle shop, up about three steps – later Mr. Powell's. Next door was Mr. Bob Smith, the baker whose smart, horse-drawn baker's cart was a well-known sight in the town. Later on, Hartley Smith, who had trained at Ward & Hubbard's in West Street, opened his radio and electrical shop next door to his father's bakery. This business was then carried on by his son, Norman. Messrs. J. & W. Baker had a large furniture shop, run by Mr. Percy Baker, lower down, opened in 1925, rebuilt 1938. Also on this

* Flemons & Marchant, behind which was the herb business described in the History Society's first book of this series – 'Dales' Dubbin & Flemons' Herbs', published in November 1996.

[JT]

Mr. Walter Baker stands in the doorway of the packed hardware shop in Church Street, 1902 *[RB]*

side of Church Street was the fish and chip shop run by Mr. & Mrs. and Miss Howard. This was later owned by Mr. Stubbs. The whole of this part of Church Street from the historic 'Red Lion' on the corner, has been demolished in the road widening and building of the shopping quadrant, etc., right down to the Ashton School.

On the south side of Church Street were many more shops. S. Farmer & Co. moved from West Street into a double fronted shop near the cross-roads. Then Gibbs & Dandy were in the premises formerly belonging to Lockhart's and which connected with their shop in High Street South. The old Drill Hall, where the Salvation Army had its first headquarters in the town, was used by Mr. Wm. Rixson as a store for his antique furniture and is now 'The Book Castle', owned by Paul Bowes. We are indebted to Paul for publishing so many interesting books on local history. Mr. W. Alfred King, trading as the Bedfordshire Supply Co., had his clothing shop next door. Mr. Tearle, father of Lewis Tearle, so well-known for being Charles Allcorn's right hand man, had his tailor's shop lower down and then Wm. Rixson his antiques shop, where many good bargains could be found. This very old building, formerly a farmhouse, was fortunately saved from demolition and is now an Italian restaurant. Retained is the original period facade with four outside steps and handrail leading up from the pavement.

Mr. Henry Janes, with his sons Bert and Frank, came next and passers by could always see them busy at work repairing customer's boots and shoes. Then there was J & W. Baker's hardware shop, opened in 1902 when Mr. Joseph Baker left a similar shop run by Mr. W. Francis when the International Stores building was divided into two shops — the International having the half next to Joseph Andrews and Mr. Francis the half next to Church Walk. Mr. Francis was no respecter of property, knocking 4" nails into a beautiful mahogany handrail from which to hang stock. Mr. Walter Baker's sons were both in the business, Reg concentrating on the hardware side and, as I have mentioned, Percy on the furniture side across the road.

Albert Smith had his sweet and tobacco shop next door, where his wife seemed to do most of the serving. Boys in Miss Harris's class, a very kind teacher at Ashton School, were often sent to Mr. Smith's for some butterscotch gums. Charlie Goodman's, another sweet and tobacconist, was lower down and then Miss Rose Johnson, a very kind, gentle lady with her companion Miss Buckle, who was always laughing. They had a little grocer's shop, entered by stepping down one or two steps from the pavement and this was another shop which gave warning of customers entering by the opening of the door ringing the bell above it. Just below was Mr. Stebbing, another tailor and a very gentle man.

I have really remembered most of the shops mentioned as they were in the 1920s and earlier, although I have strayed a little. Some, however, established in the thirties were a big asset to the town. Among these were Mr. J.B. Stevens, who ran a very successful ironmongers, and Mr. A.L. Chattell, who bought 'Cycles and Wireless' and then concentrated on wireless and television, trading in his own name. Both these shops were in High Street North.

Fred, you've given us a mine of information. When you consider the variety of shops there were in Dunstable – basically we have really covered the busy centre of the town, – elsewhere, tucked away, there were other excellent shops serving the community, weren't there?

Yes, and I have probably omitted several shops which many would think were worthy of mention. Since then, of course, and in these days of large supermarkets, a great many have closed and will never re-open, and the town will have lost a wide variety of interesting shops and colourful personalities. A very large number of the shopkeepers I have mentioned or would like to have mentioned made an invaluable contribution to the life of the town in a great variety of ways – its Civic life, as apart from the Mayors I have referred to there were the Town Councillors, Aldermen, and Justices of the Peace; to its cultural life in the town's many organisations, and in Church life, serving with dedication and very effectively in all its avenues of service. We honour their memory.

Special Notice.

Dunstable Shopping Festival.

During this week only we are giving

A Special Reduction of 3s in the £ Discount

On all Goods purchased. Delivery free.

We hold a very Large Stock of all kinds of both

New & Second-hand Furniture,

LINO, RUGS, CARPETS, &c.,

At the lowest prices obtainable in the county.

Come, see for yourself and be satisfied.

Latchford & Stairs,

HOUSE FURNISHERS,

HIGH STREET SOUTH, DUNSTABLE.

CAMPBELL, GRAVES & COX.

Let SHOPPING WEEK mean the week you shop. We are celebrating the occasion with a SPECIAL OFFER of a tremendous selection of LADIES WINTER COATS. All Sample Models, every one different. At ENORMOUS REDUCTIONS off their usual price. You will be pleased to see them. We shall consider it a pleasure to show them.

94-96, HIGH STREET,

DUNSTABLE.

Advertisements in connection with the Dunstable Shopping Festival, October 1927. [DG]

* * * * *

The caption written on the photograph says 'Section of the Dunstable market, sale by Mr. C. Allcorn', and the date would appear to be December 1913. An early photograph, therefore, of this century, before the permanent cattle pens were erected. Mr. Allcorn can be seen, centre, in bowler hat and standing on a rostrum. [MJN]

DUNSTABLE CATTLE MARKET

Don Kemp

THE START

The Dunstable Cattle Market ceased to exist in September 1955 and so ended a long established and traditional part of the life of the town. It all started with the Dunstable Charter of 1221, when one of the earliest sets of Bye-Laws stated a market could operate in the town for the sale of cattle, swine and sheep. A proviso added that all straw, dung and rubbish was to be cleared away from the site at the end of every day's trading.

The twelfth century had seen the foundation of the town among a forest region which had tracks running South to North and East to West and at these cross-roads the small market town began to develop. The area around had many small-holdings and with cattle and sheep grazing on the Chiltern Hills, marketing became part of the heritage and indeed an essential business of the town.

Twice weekly markets and several annual fairs persisted without much alteration until the middle part of the nineteenth century. The men from the small holdings, the shepherds and anyone with livestock to sell, barter or exchange would walk their stock to an area around Friary Field and the Recreation Ground a day before the market, rest overnight with their animals and then on to the market site next morning. The site consisted of rough poles in the ground to which the stock would be tied until buyers came to do their dealing.

Towards the middle of the 19th century the non-food producing population in the new industrial towns was increasing, so markets expanded and produce had to be transported. With livestock this was done by making the animals walk. Dunstable saw many enormous herds, flocks and droves passing through on the way to Smithfield, etc. Then, of course, the droving routes were replaced by rail transport and the introduction of railways meant that animals no longer lost weight en route. So with the introduction of the Markets and Fairs Acts in 1887 and 1891 small markets like Dunstable became more formal, although it did take some time to persuade many farmers that all livestock should be weighed at public market. Dunstable had in fact installed their new weighing machine in the market place in May 1888. This weighbridge had a capacity of 30cwt, with a platform 8' 6" long and 3' 6" wide. The platform was within the cattle pens with the weighing mechanism outside near the pavement. (This weighbridge was renewed in 1945 and eventually advertised for sale by the Council in 1955 when the market closed).

LATE 19th to EARLY 20th CENTURIES

The market was situated on The Square in High Street South. Always known as The Square, it is actually the triangular area from the end of the shops in Middle Row to the corner of Friars Walk. In the middle of the 19th century it consisted of small, permanent, wooden post and rail pens. This changed over the years, with extension and improvements constantly being made.

It eventually became a series of seven large permanent cattle pens of wooden posts linked with steel tube rail construction. It covered the area from Norton Court, where in pre-war days Mr. T.C. Flory had his Clifford Engineering Works and where next door was the Noah's Ark Café, southwards to where the M & W Store and the Fitness Centre are today, previously cottages and a small shop occupied by Mr. Jack Coffee, which later became the Café run by Mrs Dolly Beeson. The cattle were unloaded at the Noah's Ark end and reloaded for despatch at Dolly Beeson's end.

The ground surface was made up of 4" square granite setts, which facilitated easier cleaning down after the market. The pens for the sheep and pigs were erected on the roadway slightly north of the cattle pens, in front of what today is the T.S.B. Bank. These were not permanent pens, just sufficient being erected each week to accommodate the numbers of stock expected. Pre-war a type of wattle frame was used, tied together to form the enclosure. Later a more stronger, wooden hurdle type structure was erected, each hurdle 6ft long by 3ft high (approximately 2 metres by 1 metre). These hurdles, tied with binder twine, were assembled each market day into pens and taken down at the end of the market business for storage at the rear of the 'Saracens Head' hotel.

The market then had changed over the centuries and in the latter part of the 19th century and into the early 20th century, Dunstable held its small cattle, horse, sheep and pig market each Wednesday.

The cattle market site was Council owned and the marketing operation was always in the hands of the auctioneer who ran the business from the double fronted office situated at no. 76, (later renumbered to no. 22) High Street North at the corner of Nicholas Lane. In 1861, Mr. William Paxton Reading Southam was in charge (he was also Registrar of Births and Deaths at that time). Later a Mr. F.T. Scroggs occupied the premises and ran the market operations, and by the end of the century and up to 1912 the business was in the hands of Mr. John Holman Thorpe. It was in that year, 1912, that Mr. Charles Arthur Allcorn, who had been articled in Tunbridge Wells, bought the business and ran it most successfully for the next 50 years.

In the window of his well known offices could be seen posters advertising the Auction Sale of fat and store stock at the Cattle Market every Wednesday, commencing at 2 p.m.

On Ash Wednesday, and the second Wednesday in May, August and November, special horse markets were held and attracted a large amount of stock and an even larger number of buyers. These special markets were, however, discontinued in the early twenties with the advent of the motor car. So into the 1930s and thereon for the next year or two it was just a small town market catering for the local farmers and butchers. Some animals were brought in by small cattle wagons, or by small trailer behind a car, and some were still brought in on the hoof.

The Cattle Market was not used solely for the sale of cattle, sheep and pigs, for on two or three occasions during the year, in the pre-war era, Exmoor ponies would be offered by auction. About two dozen wild ponies, which had been rounded up in the Exmoor National Park area and transported by rail, would arrive at the Tavistock Street railway siding. After unloading they would be run along High Street North and up Chiltern Road, then along Victoria Street and Icknield Street to the Bull Pond Lane track — for that's all it was in those days, 'an unmade road, muddy in winter and dry and full of ruts in summer' as so readily described in *'Old Trades of Dunstable'*, book one. The ponies would arrive on a Monday morning and after their trip through the streets would rest for a day in a meadow belonging to Mr. Ralph Holland's farm in Bull Pond Lane, near to the top of Garden Road. On the Wednesday, Market Day, they were trotted back, and down Friars Walk to the market pens and then sold. They were purchased by farmers or for riding schools and also by local people who had children and were fortunate enough to have a field or paddock facilities to stable them. The sale price would vary, but generally finished at anything from £4 up to £10 per pony. Always a popular episode in the market's history and always in demand, the ponies usually went to good homes, and after the problem of 'breaking them in' was overcome, many could be seen trotting around the villages between the shafts of small carriages, etc.

PRE-WAR DAYS & FAT STOCK SHOWS

Another pleasant weekly diversion in pre-war days in the north of the town was the Sunday evening herd of cattle, steadily walking along the A5 from Hockliffe, through the Chalk Cutting, to the railway siding in Tavistock Street. Locals on their Sunday evening walk after Church or Chapel would go to the area and stand and watch this event. The limited amount of traffic leading north would be held up in Dunstable whilst southbound trafic would follow the herd from Hockliffe. The skill of the cattle drovers in keeping the animals together was often admired, although on some occasions a few rogues would deviate from the allotted path and escape up Beale Street, Chiltern Road or Park Street and cause some merriment in

WEDNESDAY NEXT.

DUNSTABLE

CHRISTMAS FAT STOCK SHOW.

MR CHAS. A. ALLCORN

Begs to announce that this

SHOW & AUCTION SALE

Will be held on

WEDNESDAY, 6th DECEMBER, 1922,

When there will be offered for sale about

53 CATTLE (including 30 in the Show),

90 SHEEP (including 54 in the Show),

70 PIGS (including 50 in the Show),

also a good entry of dead POULTRY, including Fowls, Ducks, Geese and Turkeys.

The Sale will commence with the Show Cattle at 12.30 sharp.

Catalogues can be had of the Hon. Secretary and Auctioneer, at the "Auction and Estate Offices," Dunstable.

[DG]

their antics and methods of avoiding capture and ultimate return to the main herd.

The cattle, and in summer months the number would be over 200, would start their journey from Trinity Hall in Hockliffe, the farm of the well known cattle dealer, Mr. George Bunker, who was the Managing Director of Bunker & Co. They would be heading for the wholesale market at Smithfield in London, via the big slaughterhouse in Islington. These animals would of course have been sold direct from the dealer to the wholesaler; this practice was quite permissible pre-war. Loaded up in cattle wagons on the Sunday evening, the 'Cattle Train', as it was known, would generally leave during the evening on its journey to London.

A special day for the market and town was held every December. This event had started in 1901 as the Christmas Fat Stock Sale. Cattle, sheep and pigs reared for the Festive Season trade were brought into market and sold by auction to local butchers and others in the surrounding areas.

Sales such as these continued until 1922 when the Dunstable Farmers Union, under the guidance of Mr. Allcorn as Secretary, inaugurated the Dunstable Christmas Fat Stock Show. It was on the first Wednesday in December 1922 that the 1st Fat Stock Show and the 22nd Fat Stock Sale, was held, and comprised Livestock Cattle, etc., and also Live Poultry. Cattle belonging to Mr. Bunker at Hockliffe fetched a price of about £55 per head, while sheep were sold for £9.2s.0d and pigs £12 each. The Show proved to be quite a success and at the Fat Stock Show dinner held that same evening it was unanimously decided to continue this as an annual event.

On 10th December 1930, the 9th Annual Show, 53 Prime Cattle, 63 Fat Sheep and 81 Hogs and Porkers were entered. It had been agreed during that year, due to the popularity and growth of the Show that a separate day should be set aside for the Live and Dead Poultry Show to be held. This show by now had classes for Live and Dead Poultry and for Rabbits and Eggs etc., and on Wednesday 17th December 1930, 523 Live or Dead Fowls, Turkeys, Geese and Ducks and numerous Rabbits, etc. had all been entered in the various classes. This event was held in a large covered building at the rear of Dolly's Café and the cottages which fronted on to the cattle pens. The building was in daily use as an engineering workshop and was owned by Messrs. Ben and Albert Scott, whose very successful garage business operated from opposite the Market, on the east side of High Street South. With their kind permission the building was loaned for this one special day every year and gratitude for this was duly noted in the reports and records of the Show.

CHAS. A. ALLCORN, F.A.I.,
AUCTIONEER, VALUER,
Estate and Transfer Agent.

ESTATES MANAGED, RENTS AND TITHES COLLECTED, INCOME TAX RETURNS PREPARED, SALES BY AUCTION OR PRIVATE TREATY, VALUATIONS MADE FOR ALL PURPOSES.

SALE of FAT & STORE STOCK
IN
DUNSTABLE MARKET
EVERY WEDNESDAY, at 2 o'clock.

Agent to the Chief Insurance Companies.

"THE AUCTION AND ESTATE OFFICES,"
DUNSTABLE.

TELEPHONE: 41 DUNSTABLE. Telegrams "ALLCORN, DUNSTABLE."

[DG]

It is also recorded that a Special Prize of One Guinea was donated by Mr.W.A. Small, a Furniture Dealer in High Street North, for the best entry in the Live Poultry Class in the Show. The winner in 1930 was Mr. William Gibbard, whose Corn Merchant's shop was another of the businesses in High Street North. The *Dunstable Gazette* at the time noted that, owing to the acute depression in the Agriculture and Farming business, the Show Committee decided not to hold the annual dinner after the Show that year.

The Show continued with ever growing success until 1938. It had become a prime annual event and many people from town and village for some miles around would visit and enjoy the Dunstable Show each December. The last Show in Dunstable was in fact held in 1938.

On the first of the Show days, the Cattle, Sheep and Pigs section was held and from early morning the farmers and their stock would arrive. The cattle in their respective pens, with straw underfoot and all being cleaned, combed and groomed were awaiting the judges. The pigs and sheep were also penned in their separate sections and would also be receiving their grooming treatment, waiting to be judged. The judges were often expert farmers in the rearing and breeding of the various classes of animal and had been brought in from other areas of the country. Resplendent in white coats they would walk round, inspect and mark accordingly, finally giving their verdict and awarding the red, blue or yellow rosettes, first, second and third for the different classes. Cups and prize money would be presented, generally at the dinner in the evening, to the winning owners.

On the Poultry Show day a similar pattern would be adopted, the live poultry in their cages, set out in their respective classes, the dead stock on tables all ready for their judges, and in due course their rosettes were awarded.

The stock would be auctioned on the day and the cattle, etc., would generally go on to the slaughterhouses. Some animals, however, would be 'bought in' by the people who had entered them and these would be taken back to the farms and almost certainly entered into other shows. In the early days Bunker & Co. would often be prize winners. In the years 1934/5/6 Mr. Wesley Dolemore of Ivy Farm, Tebworth, was the winner of the Championship Cup for 'Best in Show'. In 1937/8, his daughter, Miss Audrey Dolemore, who was a great supporter of Fat Stock Shows, won the same Cup with her Aberdeen Angus and Angus Cross Cattle. She would often 'buy them in' and take them on to other shows at Luton, Leighton Buzzard, Bletchley and Banbury and even further afield to markets in Leicester, Cambridge, Bury St. Edmunds, to name just a few, and she would win yet more prizes with them. They would eventually be sold at one of these markets and the selling price would have been enhanced by being a winner at so many shows. Any butcher who purchased one of the winning entries, be it cattle, sheep, pigs or poultry would proudly display the carcase in his window with the rosette duly attached, indicating that it was a winner at the Show.

At the poultry sale not only did local butchers bid and buy the stock, but many local people would also take advantage of the goods on offer. The live and dead poultry were duly inspected by the public and bidding was brisk. Many Christmas dinners were bought on that day at the Fat Stock Show Auction.

In 1938/9 there were 22 butchers' shops in the town and it is perhaps of interest to list them here :

William Barley, 70 West Street
Kate Bird, 47 High Street South
Harry Blake, 57 St. Peters Road
British & Argentine Meat Co., 29 High Street North
Fred Brookes, 101 High Street North
George Bryant, 218 High Street North
Robert Bunker, 57 Union Street

Co-operative Stores, 4 West Street
Direct Farmers Meat Supply, 29 High Street South
Eastmans Ltd., 26 High Street South
Empire Meat Co.Ltd., 21 High Street North
A.E.Fisher Ltd., 32 High Street South
Harold Hobbs, 55 Poynters Road
London & Central Meat Co. Ltd., 38 High Street South
Frank Longley, 28 West Street
Philip Mead, 98 Edward Street
Harry Tilley, 4 High Street South & 116 High Street North
George Waller, 27 High Street North
Harold Welch, 95 High Street South
White & Sons, 1 Edward Street
Ernest Arthur White, 7 High Street North.

Twenty-two butchers all making a worth while living in a small town with low population of some 14,000 at the time!

So it was, in those pre-war days, that many of these butchers went to Dunstable Market to buy the fat cattle that was available each week. Some of these local butchers had their own slaughterhouses and those who had no facility of their own contracted out to those who did. So the livestock went from market to shop.

There were, of course, special store stock sales held regularly. This was just a cattle sale, but in this instance not fat cattle for slaughter, but in fact much younger cattle sent in from farmers who had very little grass land to feed them on. These cattle were bought by other farmers who did have ample grazing land. They would be fed on through the summer and eventually brought back to market as fat cattle.

The farmers in the area, with much smaller levels of livestock, brought their animals to market on Wednesdays and these would be sold by auction to local butchers, through the procedure as previously described. So it was that a small country market assisted the butchers to obtain meat for sale in the town in the pre-war days.

THE WAR EFFORT

• Rationing, Officials and Dealers

1939 saw the start of the Second World War and that, for the next six years, was to have a profound impact on everyone's way of life and culture. All businesses had to undergo changes and among them, of course, were farming and the selling and purchasing of food and marketing. Dunstable Market was no exception and its operation changed dramatically. It may be said, perhaps, that this was the time

Telephone : Dunstable 41. Telegrams : "Allcorn, Dunstable."

Chas. A. Allcorn, F.A.I.

Auctioneer, Valuer,
Estate and Transfer Agent.

Sale of Stock in Dunstable Market every Wednesday, at 2 o'clock.

"The Auction and Estate Offices."

HIGH STREET, DUNSTABLE.

Mr. Allcorn's 'Auction & Estate Offices' in High Street North, immediately adjacent to the present Nationwide premises, where part of Halford's now stands.

[JT]

when the market came into its own, for it was to become a major contributor to the successful wartime strategy for distribution of meat supplies, not only locally, but also to extend into many towns in the South Eastern counties of England.

The Ministry of Food under the leadership of Lord Woolton as the Minister at the time, introduced rationing in early 1940. The ration of food allocated per person per week was :

4oz Bacon or Ham	2oz Butter	4oz Margarine
2oz Cheese	8oz Sugar	2/3 pints of Milk
4oz Cooking Fat	1 Egg	

together with 1s.2d. (6p in today's money) of meat (and if you were lucky and knew the butcher you had registered with well, you might get an occasional sausage or a small portion of offal).

So, with the meat, if you wanted to get more for your 1s. 2d., you selected a cheaper cut; conversely those who chose the dearer cut still got just the same value, 1s. 2d, but obviously less meat. The Government had decreed that all meat sales should be under the auspices of the Ministry of Food and no one was allowed to sell livestock for slaughter other than through a certified market.

Dunstable was one of only four markets in Bedfordshire to be given livestock certification. The others were Luton, held on Mondays, Leighton Buzzard, on Tuesdays and Bedford, on Saturdays. The only way farmers and dealers could sell their fat cattle, sheep and pigs for slaughter in Bedfordshire, and indeed throughout the country, was through these certificated markets, and the Ministry of Food purchased everything. Market officials were really employed, on market days, by the Ministry. The officials, who were appointed by the Ministry, comprised of a District Chairman of Auctioneers, who was Mr. Charles Allcorn, and a grading panel of three butchers and three farmers. The butchers were Harry Blake, Fred Brookes and Philip Mead, all of Dunstable. The farmers were Geoffrey Sherriff of Lewsey Farm, Leagrave, R.O. (Dick) Andrews of Chantry Farm, Houghton Regis (where Sundon Park Estate is now) and Bill Cripps of Manor Farm, Markyate. Every week one butcher and one farmer from the above would be the graders for all the animals in the market. The main grading panel, however, were Harry Blake and Geoffrey Sherriff, the others being first and second reserves.

It could be said that Dunstable Market had a larger share of cattle through its pens than many other markets. In the winter months when grass feeding was at its minimum and therefore not so many fat cattle for sale, there would be approximately 100/120 cattle each Wednesday. The summer months would average 350 each market day and it is recorded that the highest number reached in one day was 485 cattle. That meant, of course, 485 to be transported in about 50 lorry loads, for each cattle lorry would carry from 8 to 10 cattle. Then, after grading, the 485 had to be taken away, so it all had to be well organised.

A reader may say "Where did the dealers get all these cattle from each week?", for as already stated the dealers supplied most of these large numbers. Some local farmers did bring a few to market, but indeed it was very few. Those farmers who did not want the bother of entering stock in and the cost of transporting them to market would sell direct to the dealer. It was because of these well known dealers in the area that Dunstable became a prime select market, a fact not realised by local people at the time. Cattle would come from Bunker & Co., supervised by Toby Tompkins, a director of the company who lived at Trinity Hall, Hockliffe, and from W. Dolemore & Sons, at Ivy Farm, Tebworth, in the capable hands of Eric Ludgate. Also from Harry Randall at Battlesden, Ron Osborn at Park Farm in Tebworth, Vic Bunker at Great Brickhill and Archie Bunker at Stanbridge. All these were very well known and respected Cattle Dealers and they were known all over the South of England, from Devon and Cornwall through to Norfolk.

Dealers or farmers wishing to send their stock to market had to give fourteen days notice of such intention. This notice was submitted to Mr. Allcorn's office and there the entries would be categorised into the total number of steers, heifers, cows and bulls, then sheep, lambs, ewes and rams and finally pork pigs, baconers, sows and boars. All these details were submitted to the Ministry of Food on Thursday of each week, two weeks almost before the actual market day for which they were entered. The only category not requiring notice was calves, which could be brought into market on any Wednesday. Several calves would be seen in the pens, some only a few days old. If a cow gave birth to a bull calf especially, and the farmer wanted the milk, not the calf, then the calf would usually finish up at the market.

After collating the entries they were forwarded on to the M.O.F. and on the Friday prior to the market day, the distribution allocation order would be received. This would detail where all the livestock had to be dispatched on the day. Transport then had to be arranged and details would be discussed with the appointed Haulage Controller, Mr. Alf Styles of Leighton Buzzard. He would then ensure that sufficient road transport was available. Details of transportation by rail was discussed with the Station Master. During the war years and up to 1955, three Station Masters were involved, Mr. Holland, then Mr. Philbrick and finally Mr. Thompson. It was their responsibility to see that cattle wagons were in place at the Tavistock Street railway siding on the appropriate day.

• The Work Force

Mr. Allcorn's staff comprised of Lewis G. Tearle, Sidney A. Kempson and the writer. Then, as casual workers, were the drovers, very essential people on market day. One such drover everyone knew was Henry Charles Rollings, who lived in Downs Road. Everyone knew him as 'Tulip' Rollings, a very interesting Dunstable character. Where the nickname 'Tulip' came from is a mystery. His son told me "My father was always called 'Tulip' even when I was just a lad. I don't know were it came from and I have often wished I had asked him." Many who remember him will recall that he generally wore a flower in the lapel of the distinctive brown smock he wore when working . . . maybe there is a clue there. Another well known drover with a great deal of experience with cattle was Mr. Bill Sharpe from Hockliffe, who although an employee of Bunker & Co., worked all day at Dunstable Market helping to ensure its smooth running. Two other part time drovers came from Hitchin; one assisted with the cattle, the other attended to the sheep and pigs. They all had the drovers' tools of the trade, the big stick, but these drovers were very skilful at their jobs and never harmed any animal. These chaps would be employed at many other markets around the district.

So the team would assemble on Wednesday of each week, no matter what the weather, and in the summer months on very busy days an early start was called for.

On a day when 350 or more had been entered, business would start at 6 a.m. The first load of ten cattle would arrive and each in turn would be weighed by Mr. Allcorn standing behind the weighing machine and calling out the weights for the graders' and owners' information. The weight would be given in hundredweights (one cwt - 112 lbs) and in quarters of hundredweights. So you would hear 10-1 (10 hundredweight, 1 quarter), 11-2, 12-3 or 13 cwt called out, whatever the weight was. Each beast was numbered with two labels, one on its back and one on its left, rear side. (These labels were arranged in packs duplicated numbering 1 to 1000 and had the Dunstable Market code letters E.A.H. on each.) They were numbered up to 1000 to avoid any problem of identification, if by any chance cattle got held over at a slaughterhouse until the next market. So if the number finished one week at 350, the next week started at 351.

After the weight had been notified, the animal was graded. The grades indicated the price per cwt. that the dealer or farmer would receive and many times negotiation took place over the grade offered. A guaranteed price, possibly changing from week to week, was regularly reviewed and issued by the M.O.F. This was also seasonally adjusted, being lowest at the time of high production, i.e. summer time. The grades then had to be accepted by the owner. Grades were Super Special, Special, A+, A, A-, B+, B, B-, C+, C, C-, and Reject. If the grade was accepted, the hide was clip marked on the left rear, meaning that the hide hair was cut with scissors to show the long and short lines which were the sign of the grade (see diagram overleaf). This procedure did not harm or hurt the animal in any way, it was a permanent identification of grading and indicated that the cattle were then owned by the Ministry of Food.

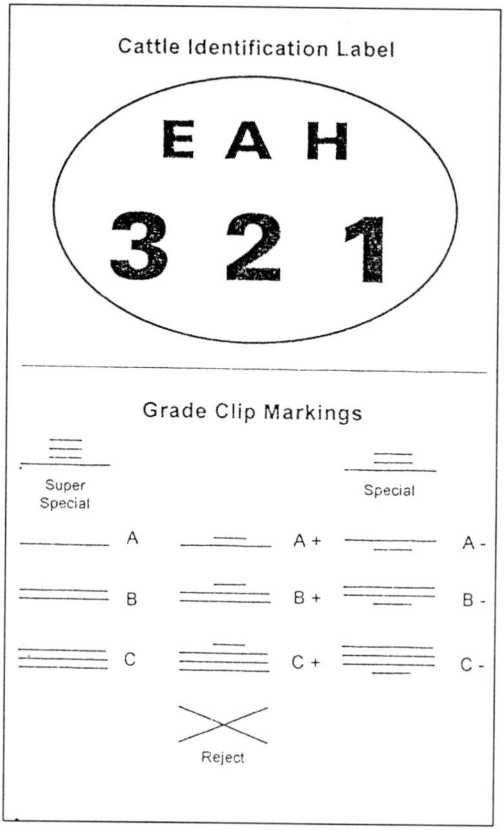

One member of Mr. Allcorn's staff would be seated on a rostrum near to the weighbridge and complete the first set of paperwork. (On wet and snowy days a large umbrella, well tied on to the rails was brought into use, to cover the books and the staff, which was very welcomed). This first form detailed the number, the owner, the colour and type of animal, the weight, the grade and whether it was bred in England, designated 'home bred' or HB, or if it had been imported from Ireland. These latter animals had a tab in the left ear and were designated TAB; the price was less for this type. This then was the procedure which continued for all the cattle.

• Typical Days & Lighter Moments

Generally the first ten animals to arrive in the morning came from Bunker and Co. and usually they were of prime quality, all Super Special. They went quickly through the system, were loaded back on the lorry that had brought them in and dispatched to the Dunstable M.O.F. slaughterhouse in Victoria Street managed by Bill Judge, of Luton, and his assistant, Sam Harris of Totternhoe. Cattle could be in the market at 6 am., graded and out by 6.30 and perhaps all slaughtered by 9.00 am. It was as quick as that.

Cattle lorries, owned by Woolwich Bros., Henry Ivory & Son, H. Jeffs, Alf Styles and others, would continue to bring in their loads throughout the day. Many, having brought ten cattle in, would then be quickly loaded with ten graded animals to be dropped off at the railways sidings before the lorry went back to the farm for yet more cattle. Movement was essential to keep the pens available.

The paperwork made out at the rostrum gave details of 20 cattle per sheet and as soon as one sheet was completed it was sent to an office room which was set up each week in the 'Saracens Head', by kind permission of Mr. Bert Cox, the proprietor at the time. As each lorry was loaded for dispatch, the numbers of the animals was noted and also passed to the office, where a dispatch note was prepared for the driver and away they went.

With 120 cattle to deal with on any one day in winter months, the outgoing allocation would probably be 20 to Dunstable, 30 to Luton (there were three official slaughterhouses in Luton — Durrant's, Fisher's and the Co-op, they would have 10 cattle each). Then 20 to Bedford (two slaughterhouses there, one in Silver Street and one in Harpur Street). The remaining 50 would perhaps go to Islington, London slaughterhouse, sometimes all by road, sometimes by rail, depending how urgently they were needed.

When the numbers reached 350 to 480, it was a vastly different allocation. Cattle were sent to towns such as Ashford, Chertsey, Chelmsford, Colchester, Croydon, Faversham, Hythe, Maidstone, Sittingbourne, Sevenoaks, Tunbridge Wells and others in the Kent and East Sussex areas. It should be remembered that especially in these areas a lot of Army camps and Air Force bases had been set up at that time. It was a war zone and troops as well as civilian populations had to be fed, so Dunstable Market played its part. The local towns, Dunstable, Luton, Bedford and even Islington were also still supplied, of course.

Some of these towns received their allocation by road, again depending on the urgency. However, many went by rail and a fairly continuous convoy of lorries would be unloading at the Tavistock Street siding all day. The station personnel did a fine job in ensuring the right cattle went in the right wagon to the right destination.

Market day was a busy day. It did have some lighter moments, the funny side. Funny, that is, depending on which way you were involved in it. Several times animals got out from the pens and would roam all over the centre of the town. (Thankfully the traffic was not so heavy in those days). Cattle would run about in the High Street, Friars Walk and Chapel Walk, anywhere it seemed to escape from the pens. Well remembered, on one occasion, was when one cow went into Mr. Herington's shop (when it was no.31 High Street South, where the Salvation Army Charity shop is today). The public watching thought this hilarious, many expecting to see the animal to come out through the window, but it walked out of the door again and continued its free run. The drovers, whose job it was to recapture these wanderers, were not so amused. However, they were very good at resolving this sort of incident, sometimes even assisted by arm waving action by members of the public, but always finally getting the animals back to the market pens.

If any of the pigs or sheep escaped from the pens, they seemed always to head off to the Friars Walk area. Often it was a matter of stopping the market activities if this happened. These animals were more difficult to catch and everyone would be involved in trying to get them penned up again. This became quite a problem as they were quickly in and out of gardens and recapture was very time consuming. Pigs were particularly difficult to recapture as they had to be manhandled back to the pens and did not always remain silent! Chaos reigned until every animal was safely back. All this was also much to public enjoyment throughout, however all were recovered eventually.

Problems also occurred when cattle jumped on another's back and caused the identification number to come off. This happened often on wet days and meant difficulties when sorting out the individual numbers of the cattle being sent away. Any cattle with no number were generally left until the end of the day. When the last loads were ready for dispatch all the documentation would be examined for details of cattle which had not gone. So the animals left would be checked for colour, type, approximate weight, grade etc., in an endeavour to ascertain the correct identification. Errors would occur with numbers as cattle were loaded, a drover could call out 321, and the person loading the cattle may write down 312. Later in the day the number 312 would come up again and a solution had to be solved as to which animal had gone where. Many times the complete consignment sent to the station had to be re-checked, and every number in every wagon reviewed.

Everything had to be right for the whole system to be accurate. For the producer, the information recorded on the weight and grade sheet served as the record for the final production of his invoice and payment certificate. For the abattoir manager, the information detailed live weight and a conversion to what should be the dead weight. For the graders, to know of the accuracy of their work when the returns came back from the abattoir. All very important for the well running of a successful market, it was therefore essential that all consignment details were accurate. The market did have regular inspection from the Ministry. The Area Supervisor, Mr Harry Mitchell, would be in attendance approximately once every two months and he would stay at the market all day. Dunstable Market was generally recorded as very efficient.

The sheep and pigs were also graded in some similar manner, although these animals were not weighed. The graders would estimate the dead weight and payment eventually made on this estimated figure. There was never an abundance of sheep or pigs in the market, perhaps 30 or 40 each market day in summer months and very less numbers in winter. The sheep were generally all sent to the local slaughterhouses, Dunstable or Luton, never on any long journeys. The pork pigs, the sows and boars would be dispatched to either Dunstable slaughterhouse or to Brazil's factory at Amersham, while the baconers would go to Letchworth or Great Missenden bacon factories.

The method used for the identification of pigs was somewhat controversial and considered by many onlookers as cruel and horrific. This was because all the pigs had their ears pierced. A large pair of clippers, with space for square metal blocks made up with ½ inch long sharp spikes in the form of letters and numbers, were used. The letters were E.A.H., again the code for Dunstable, and these were always used, together with the numbers, interchangeable according to the pen number of the pigs. The pig's left ear was pierced and in many cases caused a lot of bleeding, a sight not well received by the watching public. This piercing was the only way to identify the carcase, as after slaughter the pig would be cleaned down completely and any paint marks put on its back were soon washed away. The number pierced through the ear could be plainly seen and by this identification the correct price for the correct animals would finally get to the producer.

Very many local people would pay a visit to the Cattle Market on a Wednesday. Mothers would take their children to see the animals, especially the sheep, pigs and calves. The children loved this area. Many people will remember walking along the pavement by the market and recall the noise, the smells etc., and indeed dodging the splashes!!. Some would spend quite a time watching the activity, the unloading, the weighing, grading and the loading, some would pass on after only a short stay. All would be interested in one way or another and seemed fascinated by what was going on. It was almost a ritual for many 'to go to see the Cattle Market on a Wednesday'.

For many of the farmers the weekly trip to market provided their only point of social contact. Rubbing shoulders with fellow farmers and dealers, comparing notes and discussing events of days at other markets, all sharing their experiences and jokes over a drink in the 'Saracens Head' hotel. In those days this was indeed the only public house in the town licensed to remain open all day, for the one day a week only, on Cattle Market day. There was a certain amount of camaraderie among these farmers and dealers as they waited in very convivial surroundings, either for the next load of their cattle to arrive for grading or as they discussed the grading results they had already received. Of course, entrance to the public house was not confined to the farming fraternity only and many locals gladly took advantage of the all day opening.

The end of the activity in the market place itself brought to a close the cacophony of bleating, lowing and squealing of the animals, the clanging and banging of the gates, and the shouts of the auctioneer and the graders. The animals would all have been loaded and away, the lorries all gone. Time for the old bye-laws of centuries ago to be enacted once more. For on would come the hose pipes, brushes and shovels of the Council team as they descended on the scene to comply with the terms of the ancient Charter. By nightfall, everywhere would be clean, tidy and quiet and ready for the next Wednesday.

• Paper Work

For the Auctioneer's staff, however, only half of the work had been completed. The documentation stage was next on the list. There was always a lot of paperwork to be completed for the Ministry of Food, to enable the payment cheques to be sent on to the dealers and farmers. The Ministry insisted that all the documentation for the stock purchased at the Market on the Wednesday had to be prepared and sent to them by Thursday evening's post.

Completing the forms, therefore, started as soon as possible after the last loads had been dispatched. Market would finish between six and seven o'clock on a summer evening and work would be taken home and continue to be undertaken until midnight or even one in the morning. Then it would continue in the office all the next day.

One of the staff would deal with all relevant forms for the dealers or farmers. Every animal would again be listed with number, and full description, together with the grade and the price per cwt for its grade. The final selling price would be calculated from a laid down formula of price levels sent from the Ministry for the individual grades. These prices would vary from time to time and from season to season depending on the then current market forces. Each sheet made out would relate to up to twelve animals, so some weeks Messrs. Bunker and Co. could well have anything up to twenty sheets to cover their sales. The total amount shown on every sheet would then be collated onto the final sales summary sheet.

Another of the staff would be concentrating on the forms for the various slaughterhouses, again calculating prices and working out from the live weight and the given grade, exactly what the estimated dead weight of each beast should be. A full completed consignment note was sent out to every slaughterhouse that had received stock from the market. The totals of all this information were also collated on an abattoir summary sheet. It was these two sets of summary sheets which had to balance completely, to the penny, at the end of the day. There were no calculators, only ready reckoners available, and one learned to carry out the additions needed very well and speedily. If the totals failed to balance, and there were occasions when they did not, the work of checking carried on until any errors were found and everything was correct. It was long and very interesting work and most rewarding if all the figures balanced first time.

As a matter of interest the prices in the 1940/50s for steers and heifers weighing about 12 cwt and of the top range of grades would be between £50 and £60 each. In the years 1996/7 the prices would be in the region of £800 and £900 each.A similar procedure and sets of forms were also completed for the sheep, pigs and calves, and all the documents to the Ministry and to all the abattoirs concerned were posted every Thursday evening, although sometimes a little later than others.

By the following Wednesday, one copy of the slaughterhouse listing would be returned to the Auctioneer and would detail the actual dead weight of each animal. This information was very carefully scrutinised by the Auctioneer and the Grading Panel and gave the acknowledgement of the competency and accuracy of the graders' work the previous week. Many of the dealers would enquire how much the carcase of certain animals had weighed, thinking it might have been graded higher, but the percentage figure for correct results was excellent and very few arguments ensued from the 'inquest'.

There was also in effect a system which provided for any animals which became injured or ill on the farm. These were dealt with under what became known as the Casualty Scheme. Farmers would notify the Auctioneer's office giving details of the injured or ailing animal, be it cattle, sheep or pig, and receive instructions to take it to the Dunstable slaughterhouse. If the carcase proved fit for sale through the butcher's shop, payment would be made to the owner based on the dead weight, again after the necessary documentation had been completed. If the carcase was found to be unfit for sale it would be condemned and covered in a purple dye and eventually collected by specialist contractors who were controlled by the Ministry to remove all condemned carcases. There were times when some of these carcases went to Whipsnade Zoo for animal food. The farmer would receive just a minimum, laid down payment based on 'reject' price listing.

It is perhaps a good time to inform the reader that, as in the present day, every carcase in any slaughterhouse had to receive a health clearance through the local Health Authority. The Meat and Food Inspector would regularly visit the abattoir and thoroughly inspect every carcase and give clearance before it was sent to the shop. Any whole or part of a carcase which was considered unfit was immediately condemned and cut down, falling to the floor and covered with the dye to avoid any possibility of it being used in the butchers' shops. The Inspector was, to give him the full and correct title, the Senior Sanitary Inspector and Meat and Other Food Inspector. In 1939 it was Mr. Alf Bishop, who lived in Priory Road, and in 1941 Mr. Harold Stew, who was to become well known in Dunstable, took over this specialised work, not only looking after the meat, but covering all the food shops, milk sampling and also all matters relating to health in the town. On many occasions he would be working very late hours at the slaughterhouse examining and approving or otherwise, carcases of all the animals slaughtered there during the day. Inspection had to be carried out within a certain period of time after slaughter, so late hours working was called for.

After Mr. Stew had approved and stamped the carcase, it would be passed on for sale to the butcher. The amount of meat any butcher was allowed to purchase was dependent on the number of customers who had registered with him for their meat ration. This was done by presenting the ration book to the butcher, who extracted

May 1947, the first post-war year. The market still brings onlookers. The immediate lorry on the right in front of Scott's belongs to H.G. Ivory, otherwise Alf Styles' 'Transport for Cattle' vehicles dominate. Traffic gets away from the cross roads, past the former Belisha Beacon outside Boots. [DTC]

the relevant coupons and the total then gave the value of the meat available to him. All the supplies to the butchers were weighed and entered on advice notes and copies of these would then go through to Mr. Allcorn's office. There the prices were calculated, invoices prepared and sent out to the individual butchers. Payment was made into the office on Monday of each week and the total monies then paid on to the Ministry of Food. With these payments back to the Ministry the complete financial circle was accomplished, again enabling payments to be made to the suppliers.

Thus behind the facade of the double fronted offices at no. 22 High Street North the whole meat distribution was co-ordinated. The grading and purchasing from farmers and dealers, and the dispatching for slaughter of the livestock through the Cattle Market, followed by the sale to butchers and ultimately to the public of all meat requirements. This, then, was just another of the necessary war time effort activities within Dunstable which were taken for granted and accomplished without much publicity.

The action described continued each week. Problems did occur, of course, when an outbreak of Foot and Mouth disease in cattle was reported, for instance, as it did in those days, and movement restrictions were imposed. Only cattle within a range of some fifteen miles could be received into the market and all had to be dispatched to slaughterhouses within the same range. Then if a swine fever outbreak was reported within our area all movements of pigs was also restricted. All these sort of problems had to be sorted and although a great nuisance factor was evident at the time, with the co-operation of everyone concerned they were overcome.

THE BEGINNING OF THE END

With the ending of food rationing on 3rd July 1954, a new livestock marketing system was introduced and the Dunstable Cattle Market became a Certification Centre for the newly established Fatstock Guarantee Scheme. The introduction of the scheme brought about a dramatic change to the work at the Market. The numbers of cattle dealt with dropped back to pre-war quantities and very few sheep and pigs came to market. Farmers and dealers could, if they wished, sell to wholesalers or butchers direct without going through any Auction Market and many opted to do this.

The new Guarantee Scheme was designed to provide deficiency payments to suppliers selling cattle and sheep through livestock markets or direct to slaughterhouses. The Government of the day ran what was then known as a 'cheap food policy' enabling U.K. consumers to buy meat and other foods at world price levels. The meat prices were in general too low to support U.K. farmers, who therefore required some other form of income support. This was then provided through the deficiency payment scheme which attempted to bridge the gap between the average market price recorded for any week and the average price set by the Ministry for that week.

Broadly speaking the Fatstock Guarantee Scheme worked as follows. When stock were delivered to market they were graded to determine whether or not they met the conditions for payment of the subsidy The grading was still carried out by Messrs. Blake and Sherriff and as far as cattle were concerned only steers and heifers qualified, i.e. breeding stock were excluded. Cattle that met with the relevant criteria were marked with a conspicuous paint mark on the shoulder so that buyers at the subsequent auction would know that they had qualified for the guarantee.

During the Auction sale, the usual records, giving type, weight, price etc., were prepared and after each qualifying animal was sold it had a hole punched though its left ear. As stated the guarantee could be claimed on animals sold at the live auction and on those sold direct to abattoirs (all had to be graded). Some buyers at auction might keep the animals for some time before slaughter (many dealers buying stock would take them back to the farm to put more weight on them before slaughter). So the punched hole through the ear was a permanent identification that the guarantee had been claimed at the live market stage and it could not be claimed a second time at slaughter.

As in the war time scheme not all markets were Certification Centres. The whole process required a certain amount of staff input, so markets with low throughput began to suffer. It soon became apparent that Dunstable could fall into this category. The numbers of cattle now coming to the market were very low compared with all the previous years. The grading and auction procedure, starting at 2 o'clock on Wednesday was now generally completed by 4 o'clock, and in winter months the finish was even earlier.

CLOSURE

As far back as 1947 the Dunstable Town Council was discussing re-locating the cattle market. The editorial in the then *Dunstable Borough Gazette* of Friday 30th May 1947, under the heading 'Market Must Continue', reported 'The decision of the Town Council that the cattle market must move from The Square was overdue. It is an anomaly in a progressive town. We have gone a long way from the days when life moved so leisurely that livestock fairs in main streets were part of it. In small market towns urban and rural interests are closely linked, but in Dunstable the link has worn thin'. But the *Gazette* concluded 'In these days when the Ministry of Food are the sole purchasers of livestock for meat supplies, the market

July 1955, a month before closure. Charles Allcorn stands by the cattle pens and does what he had done for 43 years – carries out the auction. At his side, right, is the author of the narrative, Don Kemp. A well dressed man and a small boy look on. [DG]

is a vital part of the food organisation of the country and the Council cannot wash their hands of it'.

The topic was continually raised at several Council meetings over the years, but the Cattle Market, likewise, continued through the years. However, with the end of rationing in 1954 the Council became more adamant in its resolve to move the market to a new site. Plans were drawn up and tenders requested for the erection of a new cattle market in Tavistock Street, near the railway siding.

To allow the market to continue on The Square until the alterations were completed Mr. Allcorn offered to pay for the changes. This offer was accepted by the Council, who agreed on condition that the Auctioneer repaid the whole of the cost of the proposed new market site.

By the middle of 1955 the Council had received three tenders and one from Messrs. C. Firbank & Sons amounting to about £4000 was accepted. Mr. Allcorn was duly informed and during consultations with Corporation officers he contended that the proposition was entirely uneconomic from his point of view, and one he had not visualised when the arrangements were agreed in principle the year before.

Mr. Allcorn issued a statement to the Council which said; 'We understand that the cost of the proposed new market is as follows: Erection of market £4,300; cost of site £600. In addition the provision of office accommodation and other incidental work would be several hundreds of pounds thus bringing the total cost to considerably over £5000. When the scheme was under discussion some 12 months ago it was not anticipated that the cost would be anything approaching such a figure. It must also be remembered that the Council's conditions were that the Auctioneer should pay the whole of the cost, but that the market would still remain the property of the Corporation, as well as the Charter Rights'.

The statement concluded 'Before the introduction of the new marketing system in

July 1954 it was anticipated that, in addition to the fatstock coming to the market for sale there would be a fair amount of fatstock coming for private certification only. It has been found, however, that the private certification of stock has practically ceased, due to the fact that prices of cattle in particular have been so high that the collective payment made to stock so certified has been very small. Indeed, at one period it was nil. In these circumstances, owners have not been taking their stock to markets for private certification'.

The Council's General Purposes Committee, chaired at that time by Cllr W.J. Gadsden and with members such as Ald. W.T. Lack, and Cllrs P.J. Pugh, H.W. Richards, L. Palmer and L.C. Worby, replied that unless Mr. Allcorn agreed to the terms and conditions laid down by the Council within seven days, the Council would reserve the right to abandon the market 'as soon as it is practicable for them to do so'.

The Ministry of Food's certificate of approval of the livestock market as a livestock certification centre expired on 30th June 1955. Cattle were still brought into the pens on The Square on Wednesdays and sold by auction through July and into early August, although it must be added that only about twelve cattle a week were there, a complete difference from the numbers ten years earlier.

The era came to an end on The Square on 8th August 1955 when the Cattle Market was finally closed down. Sales did continue at the Tavistock Street siding for a few weeks before closing in Dunstable completely in September 1955.

Dunstable market was not alone in closing as the number of cattle markets in this country has become less and less as the years have passed by. There are now probably fewer than 200 markets in England and Wales and no more than 40 in Scotland. The future lies in the electronic auction, a computerised system of selling fatstock. The buyers bid from computer terminals in their own offices by just pressing a button. Many claim the system more humane, as the stock stays on the farm until taken direct to the abattoir. However, the aspect perhaps overlooked is the impact the system has on the social lives of farmers and the social and commercial life of the once market towns. As one councillor said at the final decision meeting 'I hope it does not go out that if the cattle market closes down, Dunstable is no longer a market town; it is only the cattle market that is going out of business'.

So an interesting and important part of Dunstable history came to an end. The cattle pens stood empty and unused and remained visible on The Square until the early 1960s when finally tarmacadam was laid on the site. Many will recollect the cattle market. Perhaps if you walk on The Square some evenings you might still hear a gate clanging, cattle lowing, a gavel banging and an auctioneer saying those immortal words 'Going, going, gone'.

[DG]

Two photographs that catch the flavour of the market. The top one, a general scene in the early 1950s. A drover is in the pen with a bullock. Behind him Mr. Allcorn stands out, on his left Don Kemp. Personalities in the lower photo, all mentioned in the narrative, include : back to the camera, right arm on side, 'Tulip' Rollings ; the four men facing, l. to r., Eric Ludgate, Harry Blake (butcher), Geoffrey Sherriff (farmer), Bill Sharpe.

KEY TO ILLUSTRATIONS

DG	Dunstable Gazette
DTC	Dunstable Town Council
FTM	Fred Moore
JT	James Tibbett's Dunstable Guides
K	Keep's Guide to Dunstable, 1930 - 31
MJN	Mrs Monica Newham
PJB	Philip Buckle
RB	Reg Baker
WGS	Worthington Smith's *'Dunstable'*, 1904
YW	Mrs Yvonne Wooster

* * * * *